Date: 12/07/20

La Constitución de los Estados Unidos

Julie Murray

Abdo Kids Junior es una
subdivisión de Abdo Kids
abdobooks.com

Abdo
SÍMBOLOS DE LOS
ESTADOS UNIDOS
Kids

abdobooks.com

Published by Abdo Kids, a division of ABDO, P.O. Box 398166, Minneapolis, Minnesota 55439.
Copyright © 2020 by Abdo Consulting Group, Inc. International copyrights reserved in all countries.
No part of this book may be reproduced in any form without written permission from the publisher.
Abdo Kids Junior™ is a trademark and logo of Abdo Kids.

Printed in the United States of America, North Mankato, Minnesota.

102019

012020

THIS BOOK CONTAINS
RECYCLED MATERIALS

Spanish Translator: Maria Puchol

Photo Credits: Alamy, Getty Images, iStock, National Archives and Records Administration, Shutterstock

Production Contributors: Teddy Borth, Jennie Forsberg, Grace Hansen

Design Contributors: Christina Doffing, Candice Keimig, Dorothy Toth

Library of Congress Control Number: 2019944036

Publisher's Cataloging-in-Publication Data

Names: Murray, Julie, author.

Title: La Constitución de los Estados Unidos/ by Julie Murray.

Other title: US Constitution. Spanish

Description: Minneapolis, Minnesota : Abdo Kids, 2020. | Series: Símbolos de los Estados Unidos |
    Includes online resources and index.

Identifiers: ISBN 9781098200787 (lib.bdg.) | ISBN 9781644943793 (pbk.) | ISBN 9781098201760
    (ebook)

Subjects: LCSH: Constitution--Juvenile literature. | Constitutions--United States--Juvenile literature. |
    Politics and government--Juvenile literature. | Emblems, National--United States--Juvenile literature.
    | Spanish language materials--Juvenile literature.

Classification: DDC 342.7302--dc23

Contenido

La Constitución de los Estados Unidos

La Constitución de los Estados Unidos es un conjunto de leyes.

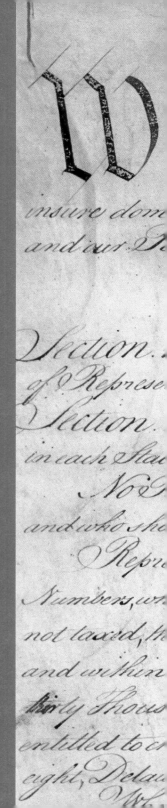

he People of the United Sta

..e Tranquility, provide for the common defence, promote the gener...

...ty, Ad ordain and establish this Constitution for the United State...

Article. I.

All legislative Powers herein granted shall be vested in a Congress...

...ives.

The House of Representatives shall be composed of Members chosen...

...all have the Qualifications requisite for Electors of the most numerous Branch...

...n shall be a Representative who shall not have attained to the Age of...

...ot, when elected, be an Inhabitant of that State in which he shall be chosen...

...tatives and direct Taxes shall be apportioned among the several States wh...

...shall be determined by adding to the whole Number of free Persons, includ...

...fifths of all other Persons. The actual Enumeration shall be made with...

...y subsequent Term of ten Years, in such Manner as they shall by Law d...

...t, but each State shall have at Least one Representative; and until such...

...three, Massachusetts eight, Rhode-Island and Providence P...

...one, Maryland six, Virginia ten, North Carolina five, South Caroli...

Las leyes son como reglas.

La gente debe seguirlas.

Tomó 116 días redactar la constitución.

La firmaron 39 **líderes**.

Ocurrió en 1787.

...tes, shall be bound by Oath or Affirmation, to support this Constitution; but no religious Test shall ever be
...le Trust under the United States.

Article. VII.

...ventions of nine States, shall be sufficient for the Establishment of this Constitution between the Sta...

done in Convention by the Unanimous Consent of the States present the Seventeenth Day of September in the Year of our Lord one thousand seven hundred and Eighty seven ar... of the Independance of the United States of America the Twelfth **In witness** whe... We have hereunto subscribed our Names,

...tary

G.º Washington — Be... and deputy from Virgi...

New Hampshire { John Langdon
Nicholas Gilman }

Massachusetts { Nathaniel Gorham
Rufus King }

Connecticut { W.ᵐ Sam.ˡ Johnson
Roger Sherman }

New York .. Alexander Hamilton

New Jersey { Wil: Livingston
David Brearley.
W.ᵐ Paterson.
Jona: Dayton }

Delaware { Geo: Read
Gunning Bedford jun
John Dickinson
Richard Bassett
Jaco: Broom }

Maryland { James McHenry
Dan of S.ᵗ Tho.ˢ Jenifer
Dan.ˡ Carroll }

Virginia { John Blair —
James Madison Jr. }

Pensylvania { B Franklin
Thomas Mifflin
Rob.ᵗ Morris
Geo. Clymer
Tho.ˢ FitzSimons
Jared Ingersoll
James Wilson
Gouv Morris }

North Carolina { W.ᵐ Blount
Rich.ᵈ Dobbs Speight.
Hu Williamson }

South Carolina { J. Rutledge
Charles Cotesworth Pinckney
Charles Pinckney
Pierce Butler. }

Georgia { William Few
... }

En ella se estableció el gobierno de los Estados Unidos. Éste se divide en 3 partes que se llaman ramas.

Ejecutiva

Casa Blanca

Legislativa

Capitolio

Judicial

Corte Suprema

Las tres ramas trabajan en conjunto. Entre todas gobiernan los Estados Unidos. Crean las leyes.

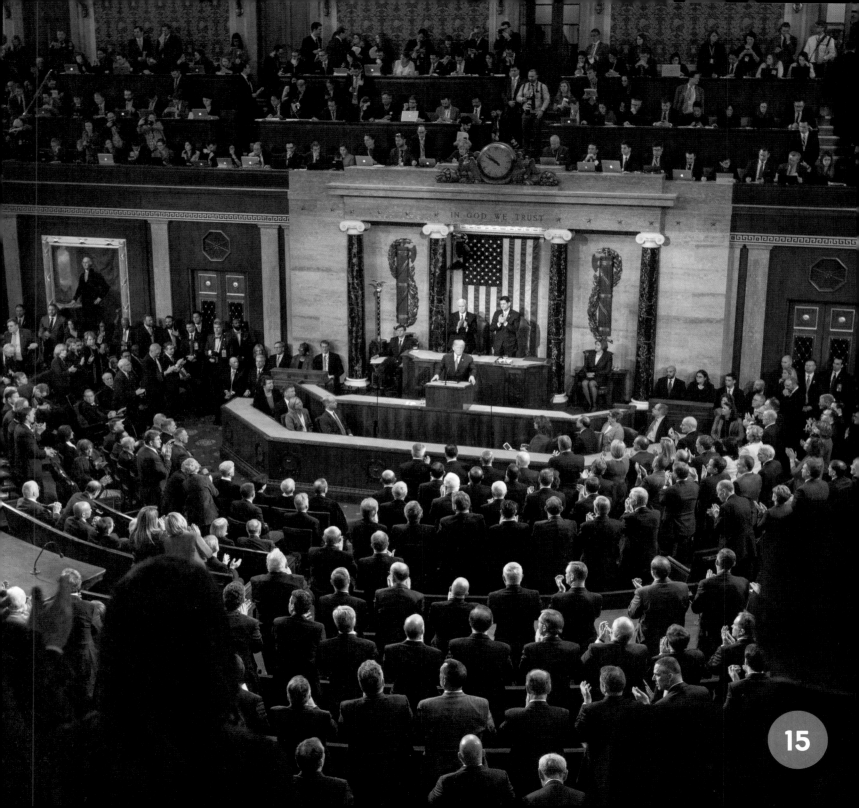

IN GOD WE TRUST

La **Carta de Derechos** fue añadida en 1791. Contenía 10 enmiendas a las reglas.

Bill of Rights

Congress of the United States,

begun and held at the City of New York, on
Wednesday, the fourth of March, one thousand seven hundred and eighty nine.

The Conventions of a number of the States having, at the time of their adopting the Constitution, expressed a desire, in order to prevent misconstruction or abuse of its powers, that further declaratory and restrictive clauses should be added: And as extending the ground of public confidence in the Government, will best insure the beneficent ends of its institution:

Resolved, by the SENATE and HOUSE of REPRESENTATIVES of the UNITED STATES of AMERICA in Congress assembled, two thirds of both Houses concurring, That the following Articles be proposed to the Legislatures of the several States, as Amendments to the Constitution of the United States; all, or any of which articles, when ratified by three fourths of the said Legislatures, to be valid to all intents and purposes, as part of the said Constitution, viz.

Articles in addition to, and Amendment of the Constitution of the United States of America, proposed by Congress, and ratified by the Legislatures of the several States, pursuant to the fifth Article of the Original Constitution.

Article the first ...... After the first enumeration required by the first Article of the Constitution, there shall be one Representative for every thirty thousand, until the number shall amount to one hundred, after which, the proportion shall be so regulated by Congress, that there shall be not less than one hundred Representatives, nor less than one Representative for every forty thousand persons, until the number of Representatives shall amount to two hundred, after which, the proportion shall be so regulated by Congress, that there shall not be less than two hundred Representatives, nor more than one Representative for every fifty thousand persons. [Not Ratified]

Article the second .... No law, varying the compensation for the services of the Senators and Representatives, shall take effect, until an election of Representatives shall have intervened. [Not Ratified]

Article the third ...... Congress shall make no law respecting an establishment of religion, or prohibiting the free exercise thereof; or abridging the freedom of speech, or of the press; or the right of the people peaceably to assemble, and to petition the Government for a redress of grievances.

Article the fourth ..... A well regulated Militia, being necessary to the security of a free State, the right of the people to keep and bear Arms, shall not be infringed.

Article the fifth ...... No Soldier shall, in time of peace, be quartered in any house, without the consent of the owner, nor in time of war, but in a manner to be prescribed by law.

Article the sixth ...... The right of the people to be secure in their persons, houses, papers, and effects, against unreasonable searches and seizures, shall not be violated, and no Warrants shall issue but upon probable cause, supported by oath or affirmation, and particularly describing the place to be searched, and the persons or things to be seized.

Article the seventh ... No person shall be held to answer for a capital, or otherwise infamous crime, unless on a presentment or indictment of a grand jury, except in cases arising in the land or Naval forces, or in the Militia, when in actual service in time of War or public danger; nor shall any person be subject for the same offence to be twice put in jeopardy of life or limb; nor shall be compelled in any criminal case, to be a witness against himself, nor be deprived of life, liberty, or property, without due process of law; nor shall private property be taken for public use without just compensation.

Article the eighth ..... In all criminal prosecutions, the accused shall enjoy the right to a speedy and public trial by an impartial jury of the State and district wherein the crime shall have been committed, which district shall have been previously ascertained by law, and to be informed of the nature and cause of the accusation; to be confronted with the witnesses against him; to have compulsory process for obtaining witnesses in his favor, and to have the assistance of counsel for his defence.

Article the ninth ...... In suits at common law, where the value in controversy shall exceed twenty dollars, the right of trial by jury shall be preserved, and no fact tried by a jury, shall be otherwise re-examined in any Court of the United States, than according to the rules of the common law.

Article the tenth ...... Excessive bail shall not be required, nor excessive fines imposed, nor cruel and unusual punishments inflicted.

Article the eleventh .. The enumeration in the Constitution, of certain rights, shall not be construed to deny or disparage others retained by the people.

Article the twelfth ... The powers not delegated to the United States by the Constitution, nor prohibited by it to the States, are reserved to the States respectively, or to the people.

ATTEST,

Frederick Augustus Muhlenberg Speaker of the House of Representatives.
John Adams, Vice-President of the United States, and President of the Senate.

John Beckley, Clerk of the House of Representatives
Sam. A. Otis Secretary of the Senate.

Se hicieron más cambios.
Uno de ellos concedió a las
mujeres el derecho a votar.

19

La Constitución está en un **museo**. ¡La puedes ver hoy mismo!

Páginas de la Constitución

Comienza así, "Nosotros, el pueblo de los Estados Unidos..."

firmas

Glosario

Carta de Derechos
enmiendas o cambios añadidos a la constitución concediendo al pueblo ciertas libertades y poniendo claros límites al gobierno.

líderes
personas que dirigen u orientan a otros. George Washington fue un líder que ayudó a crear la Constitución de los Estados Unidos.

museo
edificio donde se conservan y exponen al público objetos que son importantes para la historia, el arte o la ciencia.

Índice

Abdo Kids
ONLINE
FREE! ONLINE MULTIMEDIA RESOURCES

¡Visita nuestra página abdokids.com y usa este código para tener acceso a juegos, manualidades, videos y mucho más!

Usa este código Abdo Kids

UUK5397

¡o escanea este código QR!